THE MUSIC KIT

THE MUSIC KIT

RHYTHM READER

AND SCOREBOOK

TOM MANOFF

SECOND EDITION

W·W·NORTON & COMPANY
NEW YORK · LONDON

Library of Congress Cataloging in Publication Data

Manoff, Tom.
   The music kit. Second Edition

   Contents: [1] Workbook—[2] Rhythm reader and
scorebook.
   1. Music—Theory, Elementary. I. Title.
MT7.M267   1984   781   83-17336
ISBN 0-393-95298-3

W. W. Norton & Company, Inc., 500 Fifth Avenue, New York, N. Y. 10110
W. W. Norton & Company Ltd., 37 Great Russell Street, London WC1B 3NU

6 7 8 9 0

RHYTHM READER

CONTENTS

SCOREBOOK

CONTENTS

RHYTHM READER

CHAPTER 1

RHYTHM

Rhythm is action in time. Whether it be a drum beat, the steady ticking of a clock, or your own heartbeat, all are specific actions that occur in a space of time. Rhythmic notation is the system used to indicate the number of actions, the time each action takes, and the relationship of these actions to a *beat*. This basic beat, or pulse, is what we feel when we step in time to a marching band or tap our feet to a rock or jazz tune. The speed of the beat is described by the term *tempo*. A polka or rock dance has a fast tempo; a funeral march has a slow tempo. The rhythms we **hear** are represented by symbols we **see**, called *notes.*

THE QUARTER NOTE AND THE EIGHTH NOTE

The first notes we learn are the quarter note (♩ or ♩) and the eighth note (♪ or ♪). Quarter notes are twice as long in duration as eighth notes; conversely, it requires two eighth notes to equal the duration of one quarter note.

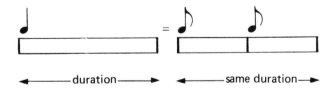

The several parts of the eighth note are the *notehead, stem,* and *flag:*

2

BEAMING EIGHTH NOTES

Eighth notes can be beamed together for easier reading.

1   Rewrite these eighth notes, using beams:

Example:

1.

2.

3.

SPEAKING RHYTHMS

To get you started reading and comprehending rhythm quickly, we use a method for speaking simple rhythms. Quarter notes (♩ or ♩) will be spoken "ta." Eighth notes (♪, ♪, ♫, or ♫) will be spoken "tee."

2   Speak in an even, steady manner, and at a moderate tempo:

ta   ta   ta   ta   ta   ta   ta   ta

Speak in an even, steady manner:

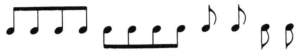

tee tee tee tee tee tee tee tee tee tee tee tee

3

1. Listen to *Rhythm 1* (S 1, B 1) a few times, then speak the rhythm with the recording. Before each exercise, you will hear a count to establish the tempo. In this case, the count is "one, two, three, four."

Rhythm 1

2. Repeat *Rhythm 1,* speaking and following this version, which is the same rhythm as the one just above, but notated differently.

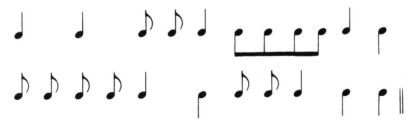

DOUBLE BAR

A *double bar* (‖ or ▐) indicates the end, as in the example directly above.

REPEAT SIGNS

A group of notes is repeated when it is enclosed by *repeat signs,* ‖: :‖ . Therefore:

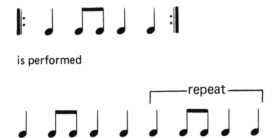

is performed

4 Write out each of these rhythms with the repeat:
Example:

1.  =

2. =

3. =

In performing a line of music, go back to the beginning without any lapse of the beat when you reach a repeat sign.

5 Speak *Rhythms 1* through *3* with the recordings. Remember the repeat signs.

1. *Rhythm 1* (S 1, B 1)

2. *Rhythm 2* (S 1, B 1)

3. *Rhythm 3* (S 1, B 1). You will hear "one, two, three" before the rhythm.

6 Repeat *Rhythms 1* through *3* with the recording. This time, speak and clap.

7 Repeat *Rhythms 1* through *3* with the recording. These versions are the same rhythms as in **5**, but notated differently. Speak and clap:

1. *Rhythm 1*

2. *Rhythm 2*

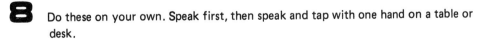

3. *Rhythm 3*

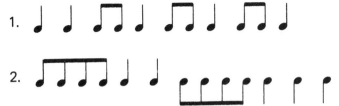

8 Do these on your own. Speak first, then speak and tap with one hand on a table or desk.

9 Tap and imagine you are speaking these rhythms. Don't speak!

FERMATA SIGN

The *fermata* symbol (⌒), when placed above a note, indicates that the note is to be held for a longer duration than its indicated value. The duration is left to the discretion of the performer. The fermata is also called a hold.

6

TERMS, SYMBOLS, AND CONCEPTS

rhythm

beat

basic pulse

duration

tempo

the relationship between ♩ and ♪

note

notehead

stem

flag

beaming eighth notes

𝄆 : ⌢ : 𝄇

CHAPTER 2

RESTS

Just as there are symbols which represent musical sounds for specific time durations, there are symbols which represent the absence of musical sound, or silence. These symbols are called *rests*. A *quarter rest* (𝄽) has the same time value as a quarter note. In the following rhythms, speak the quarter rest as "rest."

1   Speak with the recording. Do not clap.

1. *Rhythm 4* (S 1, B 2)

speak: ta   ta   rest   ta   ta   rest   ta   ta

2. *Rhythm 5* (S 1, B 2)

3. *Rhythm 6* (S 1, B 2)

4. *Rhythm 7* (S 1, B 2)

2 Repeat *Rhythms 4* through *7*. Speak and tap with the recording. Do not tap the rests, just say **"rest,"** as on the recording.

3 Repeat these new versions of *Rhythms 4* through *7*. Speak and tap with the recording.

1. *Rhythm 4*

2. *Rhythm 5*

3. *Rhythm 6*

4. *Rhythm 7*

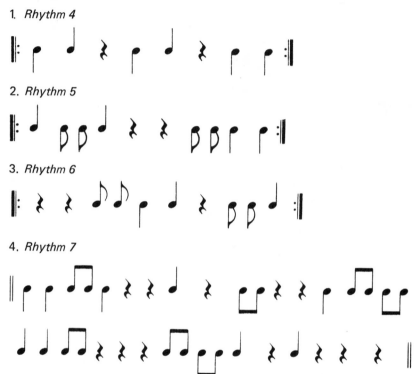

METER

We naturally hear rhythm in groups of beats. Think, for example, how often you hear a "tic" followed by a "toc." In music notation, this organization into groups of beats is called *meter*. Some common groupings are two, three, and four beats. Each group is called a *measure* and is indicated by a vertical line, called a *barline*.

A rhythm with meter (groups of 2 ♩'s)

A rhythm with meter (groups of 3 ♩'s)

A rhythm with meter (groups of 4 ♩'s)

STRONG AND WEAK BEATS

Recognizing measure divisions by ear is often the result of hearing strong or accented beats followed by weak or unaccented beats. In the following examples, the strong beat is indicated by an accent sign (>).

4 Speak these rhythms, accenting the "ta" or "tee" where indicated.

meter

METER SIGNS AND TIME SIGNATURES

The meter of a piece is indicated by a *meter sign*, or *time signature*, consisting of an upper number and a lower number. The upper number indicates how many beats there are in each measure; the lower number indicates the kind of note which receives one beat.

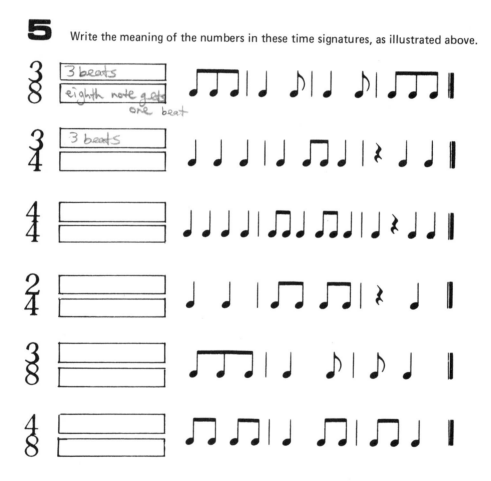

4 beats per measure
the quarter note equals one beat

The time signature above is usually spoken as "four-four."

5   Write the meaning of the numbers in these time signatures, as illustrated above.

3/8 | 3 beats |
eighth note gets one beat

3/4 | 3 beats |

RHYTHMS WITH AND WITHOUT METER

While most music you will encounter has meter, some music does not. An understanding of written rhythms with and without meter is helpful in becoming a good musician. Both types will be studied throughout this book.

COUNTING PULSES IN THE MEASURE

Now we will count the number of beats or basic pulses per measure. For example:

METRONOME AND TEMPO

A metronome is a mechanical device which supplies a basic pulse at specific tempos. For example, set a metronome at 60 and you will hear 60 even pulses per minute; set it at 100 and you will hear 100 pulses per minute, etc. A metronome marking is specified by the letters "M.M." with an indication of what kind of note is represented by the basic pulse, as in the exercises below. Access to a metronome will be quite useful for working through the *Rhythm Reader*.

 Count each of these meters with the indicated tempo determined by the metronome marking. Each spoken number must coincide with the steady pulse of the metronome.

2. Repeat Exercise 1 at M.M. ♩ = 120.

12

4.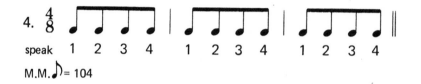

speak   1   2   3   4   1   2   3   4   1   2   3   4

M.M. ♪ = 104

7

Listen to *Rhythms 1–7* and count the meters as indicated.

1. *Rhythm 1*

count   1   2   3   4   1   2   3   4   1   2   3   4   1   2   3   4

2. *Rhythm 2*

count   1   2   3   4   1   2   3   4

3. *Rhythm 3*

count   1   2   3   1   2   3   1   2   3   1   2   3

4. *Rhythm 4*

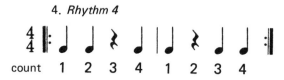

count   1   2   3   4   1   2   3   4

5. *Rhythm 5*

count   1   2   3   4   1   2   3   4

6. *Rhythm 6*

4/4 ‖: 𝄽 𝄽 ♫♩ | ♩ 𝄽 ♫♩ :‖

count   1   2   3   4   1   2   3   4

7. *Rhythm 7*

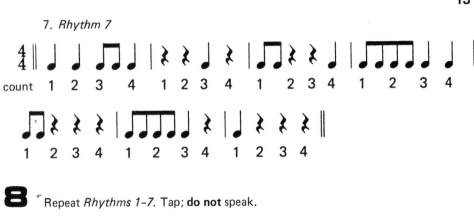

8 Repeat *Rhythms 1–7.* Tap; **do not** speak.

9 Play each of these exercises on the piano, another keyboard instrument, or the guitar (see Chapter 2 in the *Workbook*). First speak each rhythm, then play it.

1.

2.

3.

4.

5.

6.

14

TERMS, SYMBOLS, AND CONCEPTS

meter

measure

barline

strong and weak beats

$>$

meter signs/time signatures

counting the basic pulse

metronome

CHAPTER 3

EIGHTH REST

A silence equal in duration to the eighth note (♪) is the *eighth rest* (ɣ). We now know four **rhythmic symbols**:

quarter note: ♩

quarter rest: 𝄽

eighth note: ♪

eighth rest: ɣ

NOTE VALUES

If the quarter note is the basic pulse, it is given a value of one beat. The other rhythmic symbols can be measured against this quarter-note beat.

♩ = 1 beat

𝄽 = 1 beat

♪ = 1/2 beat

ɣ = 1/2 beat

1 Add up the total number of beats of each rhythm.
Example

♩   𝄽   ʳ ʳ ♫ ♩   ♪ ⎫ = 5½ beats
1 + 1 + ½ + ½ + ½ + ½ + 1 + ½ ⎭

1. 𝄽 𝄽 𝄽 𝄽 ♫   = 5½
   1   2   3   4   5 +

2. ʳ ʳ ʳ ʳ ʳ ʳ ʳ ʳ 𝄽   = 5
   ½ ½ ½ ½ ½ ½ ½ ½ 1

3. ♩ ♪ ♩ ♪ ʳ ♪ ♩   = 5
   1   + ½ 1   ½ ½ ½ 1

4. ♫ ʳ ♪ ♩ 𝄽 𝄽 ♪   = 5½
   ½ ½ ½ ½ 1   1   1 ½

5. ♩ 𝄽 𝄽 ♪ ʳ ʳ ♪   = 5
   1   1   1 ½ ½ ½ ½

6. ♩ 𝄽 𝄽 𝄽 ♪ ♩ ʳ ♩   = 7
   1   1   1 1 ½ 1 ½ 1

7. ♪ ♩ ʳ ʳ ♩ ♩ ʳ ʳ ♩ ʳ ♩ = 8
   ½ 1 ½ ½ 1 1· ½ ½ 1· ½ 1

SPEAKING THE EIGHTH REST

When speaking rhythms, say the syllable "m" for the eighth rest. When clapping or tapping a rhythm, speak each rest but don't clap or tap it. Say "rest" for the quarter rest.

2 Speak these rhythms with the recording. Do not clap. The count for *Rhythm 11* is "one, two"; the count for *Rhythm 12* is "one, two, three."

1. *Rhythm 8* (S 1, B 3)

$\frac{4}{4}$ 𝄆 ♫ ʳ ♪ ♪ ♪ ʳ ♫ | ʳ ♫ ♫ ♩ ♩ 𝄇

2. *Rhythm 9* (S 1, B 3)

$\frac{4}{4}$ 𝄆 ♩ ♫ ʳ ♪ ♩ | ♪ ʳ ʳ ♪ ♩ 𝄽 𝄇

Do More

3. *Rhythm 10* (S 1, B 3)

4. *Rhythm 11* (S 1, B 3)

5. *Rhythm 12* (S 1, B 3)

3 Repeat *Rhythms 8-12,* speaking and clapping. Don't clap the rests, but speak them.

4 Repeat *Rhythms 8-12.* This time count the meter with the rhythms, but do not clap.

1. *Rhythm 8*

count 1   2   3   4   1   2   3   4

2. *Rhythm 9*

count 1   2   3   4   1   2   3   4

3. *Rhythm 10*

count 1   2   3   4   1   2   3   4

4. *Rhythm 11*

count 1   2   1   2   1   2   1   2

5. *Rhythm 12*

count 1   2   3   1   2   3   1   2   3

USING BOTH HANDS — COORDINATION

5 Speak and tap on a table or desk.

1. Use the right hand:

2. Use the left hand:

6 Now tap with both hands at once. Tap eighth notes with the right hand against quarters with the left. Do it twice, first speaking the eighths, then speaking the quarters.

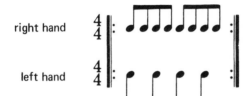

Repeat with the parts reversed.

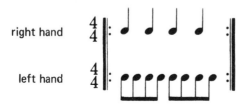

7 Tap and speak these rhythms. First start the left hand **alone.** When you have established the basic pulse, **add** the right hand. Speak the right hand part **only.** Some practice may be required for the accomplishment of these exercises.

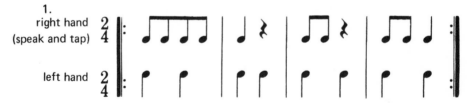

8 Tap *Rhythms 13–16* with both hands. On the recording the lower part is performed on bass drum (it starts the rhythm). The higher part is played on a snare drum. Write numbers under each measure of the bass drum part to show the meter (1 2 3 4, 1 2 3, or 1 2).

1. *Rhythm 13* (S 1, B 4)

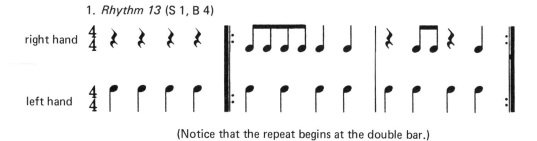

(Notice that the repeat begins at the double bar.)

2. *Rhythm 14* (S 1, B 4)

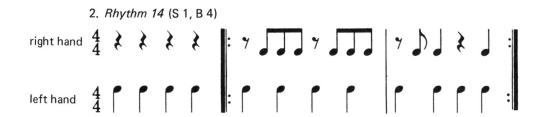

20

3. *Rhythm 15* (S 1, B 4)

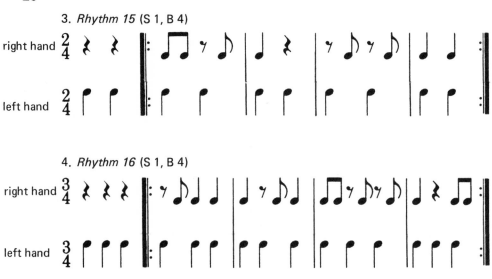

4. *Rhythm 16* (S 1, B 4)

9 Play these exercises. Speak the rhythm first, then play and only imagine you are speaking.

TERMS, SYMBOLS, AND CONCEPTS

CHAPTER 4

NOTES CONTROL SPACE

The written note (or rest) controls a space on the page in the same way that the sound it represents controls a period of time. Longer notes and rests control more space than shorter notes and rests. Observe how these notes and rests are written on the rhythm spacer below, which shows their relationship to a quarter-note pulse. The shaded part represents the amount of space that the note controls.

Rhythm Spacer

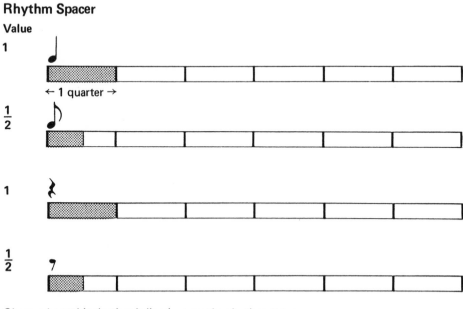

Observe how this rhythm is lined up on the rhythm spacer.

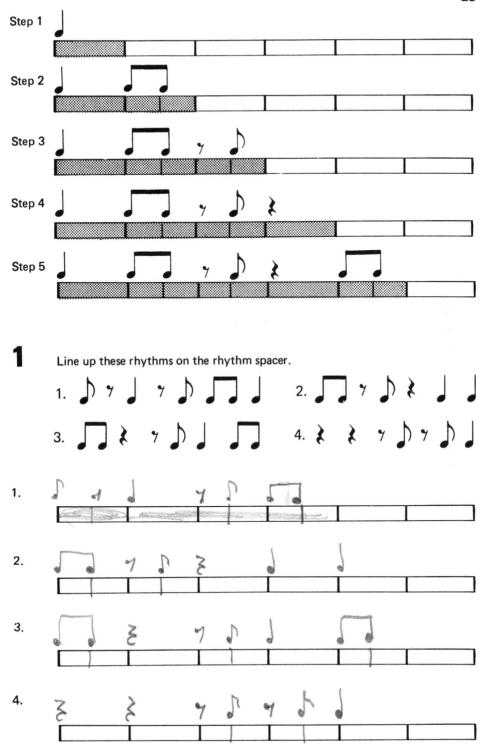

Step 1

Step 2

Step 3

Step 4

Step 5

1   Line up these rhythms on the rhythm spacer.

1.

2.

3.

4.

1.

2.

3.

4.

2 Tap and speak *Rhythms 1–12* (S 1, B 1–3). Tap with your right hand when the stems go up; use your left hand for notes whose stems go down.

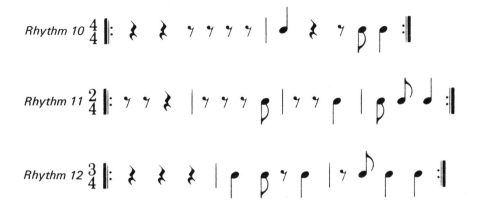

3 Turn to *Rhythms 13–16* on pages 19–20. Rewrite them in your music notebook with the parts reversed (see below). Tap with both hands while listening to the recorded versions.

Example: *Rhythm 13*—parts reversed

1ST AND 2ND ENDINGS
When an exercise or piece of music utilizes repeat signs, you may find two endings. If so, when you repeat, skip the measure or measures marked *1st ending* and go directly to the measure or measures marked *2nd ending*.

Example:

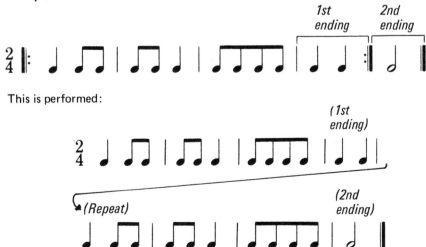

This is performed:

4 Tap:

OTHER TYPES OF REPEATS

D.C. al fine (*Da Capo al fine*: literally, "from the beginning to the end"). If you find this abbreviation at the end of a piece, go back to the beginning and repeat, stopping at the place marked *fine*.

D.S. (*Dal Segno*: literally, "to the sign"). If you find the letters *D.S.* at the end of a piece, go back to the sign (𝄋), not necessarily to the beginning, and repeat to the end.

5 Play these exercises. Speak the rhythm first, then play. Imagine you are speaking the rhythm when you play. When you play, do not speak!

6.

7.

8.

TERMS, SYMBOLS, AND CONCEPTS

notes control space
1st and 2nd endings
D.C. al fine
D.S.

Stopped

CHAPTER 5

NOTES LONGER THAN THE QUARTER NOTE

Most of the rhythms we have talked about have the quarter note as the basic pulse. We now use the quarter note to measure longer notes.

whole note	𝅝	=	♩ ♩ ♩ ♩
dotted half note	𝅗𝅥.	=	♩ ♩ ♩
half note	𝅗𝅥	=	♩ ♩

SPEAKING THE LONGER NOTES

When you reach a note longer than the quarter note, speak "ta— a— a" for as many quarters as the note equals.

1 Tap these rhythms with both hands. Notice the durations of 𝅗𝅥, 𝅗𝅥., and 𝅝. Repeat, speaking the top part.

1.

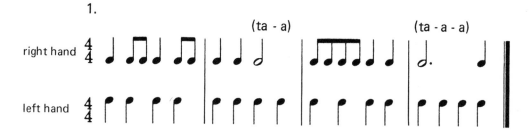

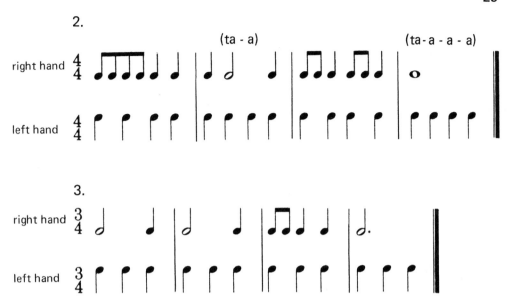

COUNTING NONMETERED RHYTHMS WITH NUMBERS

When counting nonmetered rhythms with numbers, give each note its value in quarter notes.

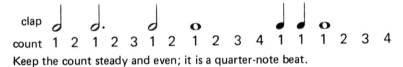

Keep the count steady and even; it is a quarter-note beat.

2 Clap and count.

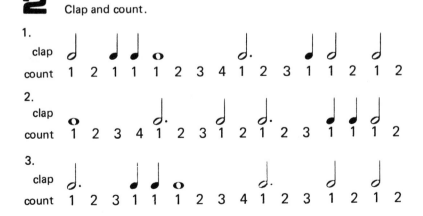

COUNTING RHYTHMS IN METER

When counting in a specific meter, you are counting the number of beats per measure. The value of each note fits into that metrical grouping.

3 Tap *Rhythms 17–20* with the recording. The top part is heard on a synthesizer (playing one pitch), the bottom is played on bass drum.

1. *Rhythm 17* (S 2, B 1)

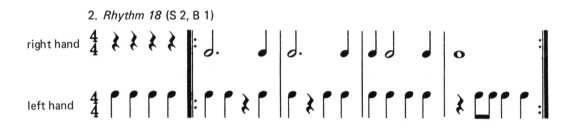

2. *Rhythm 18* (S 2, B 1)

3. *Rhythm 19* (S 2, B 1)

4. *Rhythm 20* (S 2, B 1)

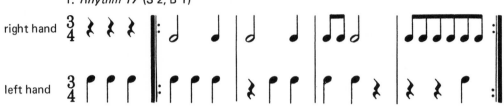

4 Clap these rhythms while counting the beats in the measure.

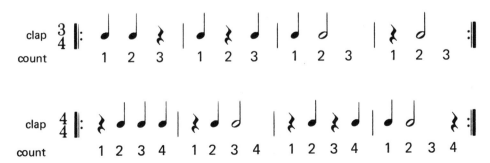

5 Clap and count these rhythms. When a rest appears, don't clap, but keep counting.

RESTS LONGER THAN THE QUARTER REST

whole rest   ▬   =   𝄽 𝄽 𝄽 𝄽

dotted half rest   ▬•   =   𝄽 𝄽 𝄽

half rest   ▬   =   𝄽 𝄽

6   Tap and count. The pulse equals the quarter note.

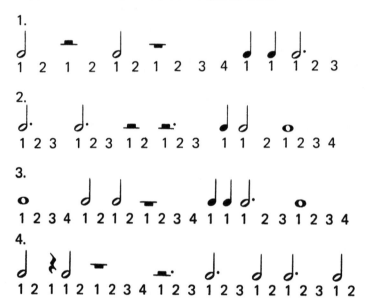

1.

1 2   1 2   1 2   1 2 3 4   1 1   1 2 3

2.

1 2 3   1 2 3   1 2   1 2 3   1 1   2   1 2 3 4

3.

1 2 3 4   1 2   1 2   1 2 3 4   1 1 1   2 3   1 2 3 4

4.

1 2   1 1 2   1 2 3 4   1 2 3   1 2 3   1 2   1 2 3   1 2

CONDUCTING

Learn the basic conducting patterns. In this way, you translate each meter into physical action. The patterns are illustrated below. The lines indicate the motion of the arm led by the hand. The motion should be free and flowing. As you develop the basic movements, count the meter.

7   Practice these basic conducting patterns:

2 basic pulses

($\frac{2}{2}$ or $\frac{2}{4}$)

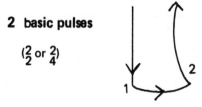

3 basic pulses

$(\frac{3}{2}$ or $\frac{3}{4}$ or $\frac{3}{8})$

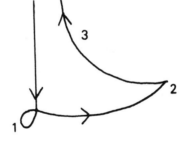

4 basic pulses

$(\frac{4}{2}$ or $\frac{4}{4}$ or $\frac{4}{8})$

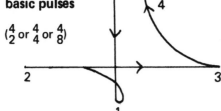

8 Play these exercises:

1.

2.

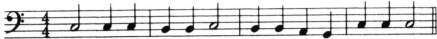

3.

4.

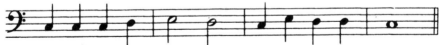

5.

6.

7.

9 Tap out the rhythms of the following songs from the *Scorebook.*

The Wraggle-Taggle Gypsies, O! (SB 15)

Philis, Plus Avare que Tendre (SB 22)

Que ne suis-je la Fougère (SB 23)

Oh, How Lovely Is the Evening (SB 28)

Shalom Chaverim (SB 31)

Sarabanda (SB 37)

TERMS, SYMBOLS, AND CONCEPTS

o   ▬

♩.   ▬·

♩   ▬

counting nonmetered rhythm

counting metered rhythm

conducting patterns (2, 3, and 4 beats)

CHAPTER 6

NOTE SYMBOLS

We start our discussion of the note system with the whole note, which may be divided into smaller notes. The symbol for each note and its equivalent rest is presented here. The duration of each note or rest in this list is half the duration of the note or rest above it.

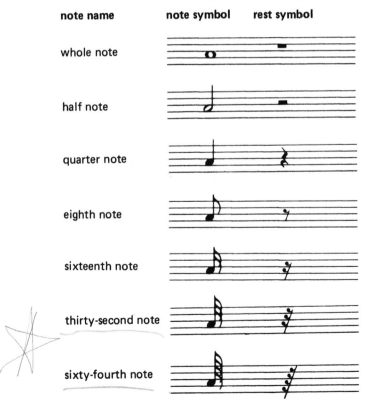

note name	note symbol	rest symbol
whole note		
half note		
quarter note		
eighth note		
sixteenth note		
thirty-second note		
sixty-fourth note		

BEAMS

Notes smaller than the quarter note are written with *flags* (♪ ♬ ♬). When a group of flagged notes are written together, unifying *beams* are used.

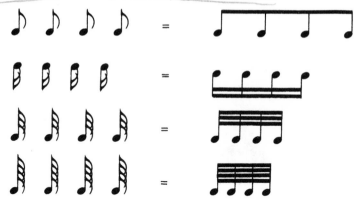

Notice that the number of flags is replaced by the same number of beams.

COMBINATIONS OF NOTES WITH BEAMS

Notes of different time values can be joined together with beams.

The beam may be on the left or right side of the note stem. It is the **number** of beams that touch the stem which determines the value of the note.

1   Rewrite these rhythms with flags:

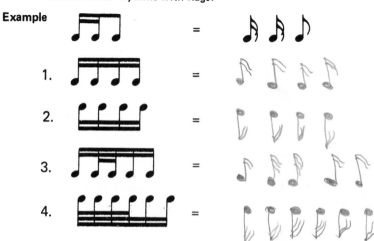

Example

1.

2.

3.

4.

THE VALUES OF NOTES IN RELATIONSHIP TO EACH OTHER

The quarter note is often used as the basic unit for measuring the values of other notes. Below, each note is expressed in quarter notes.

1. Notes larger than the quarter note:

2. Notes smaller than the quarter note are often beamed in groups equal to one quarter note in duration:

2 Write the number of smaller-value notes which equal the indicated larger-value note.

Example

THE TIE

Two notes of the same pitch may be connected with a curved line joining one notehead to the other. This line is called a *tie*. The first note is then prolonged by the value of the second.

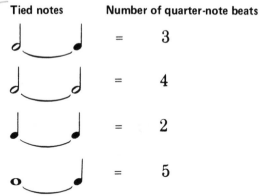

Tied notes	Number of quarter-note beats
=	3
=	4
=	2
=	5

Do not confuse the tie with a similar curved line called the *slur*, which indicates that two or more **different** pitches are to be played smoothly (see *Workbook*, Appendix II). The tie always unites two notes of the **same** pitch.

ties   slurs

THE DOTTED NOTE

You have already been using one dotted note (♩.). Any note can be dotted. A dot after a note is called an *augmentation dot.* This lengthens the note by half its own value. Note that prolonging a note with an augmentation dot is an alternative to using a tie to accomplish the same purpose.

♩.	=	♩	+	♩	also written	♩ ♩
			(half of ♩)			

| ♩. | = | ♩ | + | ♪ | also written | ♩ ♪ |
| | | | (half of ♩) | | | |

| ♪. | = | ♪ | + | ♬ | also written | ♪ ♬ |
| | | | (half of ♪) | | | |

The augmentation dot is **always** found in a space, even when the note it augments is on a line. For example:

3 With the **quarter note** valued at **one**, give the value of each of these notes or groups of notes.

Examples

𝅗𝅥. = 3   (𝅗𝅥 + ♩)
                2   1

♩. = 1½   (♩ + ♪)
               1   ½

♩. ♩. = 3   (♩. + ♩.)
              1½   1½

𝅝· = (𝅝 + 𝅗𝅥)
      4 2
	𝅗𝅥‿♩‿♩ = (𝅗𝅥 + 𝅗𝅥 + 𝅗𝅥)
	         2 1 1

𝅗𝅥‿𝅗𝅥 = (𝅗𝅥 + 𝅗𝅥)
      2 + 2
	𝅗𝅥‿♪ = (𝅗𝅥 + ♪)
	      2 ½

𝅗𝅥‿♪ = (♩ + ♪)
      1 ½
	𝅗𝅥·‿♩· = (♩ + ♩ + ♩ + ♪)
	      2 1 1 ½

♩. ♩. = (♩. + ♩.)
      1½ 1½
	♪. ♪. = (♪ + ♪ + ♪ + ♪)
	      ½ + ¼ + ½ + ¼

♪ ♪ ♪ = (♪ + ♩ + ♪)
      ½ 1 ½
	𝅝· ♩ = (𝅝 + 𝅗𝅥 + 𝅗𝅥 + ♩)
	      4 2 2 1

40

4 Write **one** note that equals each of these rhythmic groupings.

Cheek

Example		
♩ ♪ = ♩.		♪ ♪ = ♩.
♩ ♩ = ♩..		𝅝 ♩ = 𝅝.
♩ ♩ = 𝅝		♩ ♩ ♩ = 𝅝
♩ ♩ = ♩		♩ ♩ ♩ = ♩
♪ ♪ = ♪		♩. ♩ = 𝅝

5 Name each symbol and give its value with the quarter note valued at one.

♩	𝄽	𝄾	♫	𝄿	𝄼	𝅝
1	1	$\frac{1}{2}$	$\frac{1}{4}$	$\frac{1}{8}$	4	4

𝄻	𝅗𝅥	♪	𝄿	♬	𝄿	♬
2	2	$\frac{1}{2}$	$\frac{1}{4}$	$\frac{1}{8}$		$\frac{1}{16}$

D₀

6 Total each rhythmic group with the quarter note valued at one.

Example	♪ 𝄿 𝄼	= 3
	𝄿 ♪ 𝄿 ♩ 𝄿 ♪	= 3
	𝄿𝄿♪ ♫ ♩ 𝄽	=
	♪ 𝄿 𝄿 ♪ 𝅘𝅥𝅯𝅘𝅥𝅯𝅘𝅥𝅯𝅘𝅥𝅯	= $2\frac{3}{4}$

D₀

ANACRUSIS

Sometimes a piece or a rhythm will begin on the last part of the measure. This is called the *anacrusis*, or *upbeat*. The value of the anacrusis is subtracted from the final measure. Observe this practice in these two examples:

RESTS

Certain practices in writing rests are different from those in writing notes.

1. The whole rest (⬛) is used to represent a full measure of rest in any meter. It always hangs beneath the fourth line in the center of the measure.

Example

2. Rests are not tied.

3. Half rests (⬛) always sit atop the third line. They are rarely used in $\frac{3}{4}$.

4. Quarter rests (𝄽) and half rests (⬛) are usually written **on** the beat, not **off** the beat.

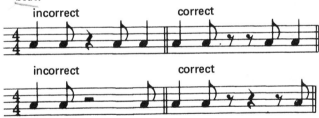

7 Play the following exercises:

3. Traditional

4. Traditional

TERMS, SYMBOLS, AND CONCEPTS

beams

flag

stem

tie

augmentation dot

slur

anacrusis or upbeat

Stopped

CHAPTER 7

SUBDIVISION OF THE BASIC PULSE

One way to aid understanding certain rhythms is to **subdivide** the basic pulse. This helps to locate the exact place where notes occur when they fall between beats. There are many ways of subdividing, and working with all of them will expand your understanding of rhythmic notation.

Common count of 4/4

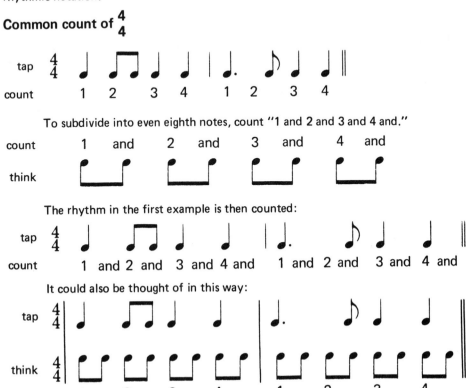

To subdivide into even eighth notes, count "1 and 2 and 3 and 4 and."

The rhythm in the first example is then counted:

It could also be thought of in this way:

44

The subdivision provides a steady eighth-note pulse by which any note off the main beats may be correctly positioned.

1 Count these meters as indicated.

1.

2.

3.

4.

5.

2 Count *Rhythms 21–23* as indicated while listening to the recording.

1. *Rhythm 21* (S 2, B 2)

— lowest subdivision is an eighth-note, so this is what you use as the pulse here

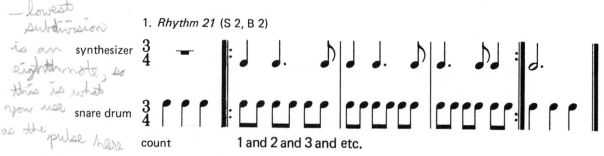

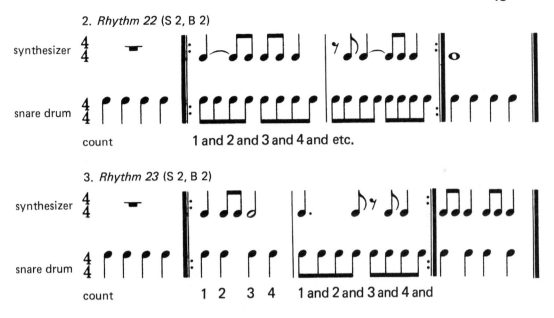

2. *Rhythm 22* (S 2, B 2)

synthesizer

snare drum

count   1 and 2 and 3 and 4 and etc.

3. *Rhythm 23* (S 2, B 2)

synthesizer

snare drum

count   1 2   3 4   1 and 2 and 3 and 4 and

3 Repeat *Rhythms 21–23* with the recording. Tap the higher part. Repeat, tapping both parts.

4 Rewrite *Rhythm 22* using dotted notes instead of ties.

5 Above the subdivisions provided, write the three rhythms given below. Then speaking or thinking the subdivision, tap the rhythm. Remember that the subdivisions must be steady when you are counting or thinking a subdivided beat.

Rhythm 1

Rhythm 2

Rhythm 3

Rhythm 1 3/4

subdivision   1 and 2 and 3 and   1 and 2 and 3 and

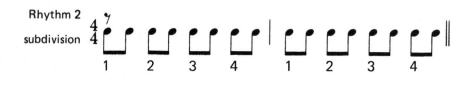

Rhythm 2   4/4

subdivision

           1   2   3   4   1   2   3   4

Rhythm 3 2/4

subdivision   1 and 2 and   1 and 2 and   1 and 2 and 1 and 2 and

6   Play these exercises.

7 Choose from among these pieces in the *Scorebook* and tap the rhythms.

The Trees They Do Grow High (SB 1)

I Know Where I'm Going (SB 2)

The Riddle Song (SB 6)

Lullaby, by Brahms (SB 8)

Dona, Dona (SB 12)

Wayfaring Stranger (SB 14)

The First Noel (SB 27)

In the following, choose one part to tap out:

Remember, O Thou Man (SB 36)

The Young Convert (SB 34)

Willie, Take Your Little Drum (SB 35)

Dona Nobis Pacem (SB 51)

The Welcome Song (SB 32)

TERMS, SYMBOLS, AND CONCEPTS

subdivision

methods for counting

CHAPTER 8

DIVISION OF THE QUARTER NOTE INTO SIXTEENTHS

The quarter note can be further divided into four parts to help understand rhythms using eighth notes, sixteenth notes, and other notes of shorter duration. When speaking, accent "one" in each group of four.

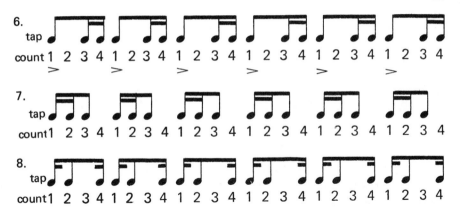

6. tap
count 1 2 3 4 1 2 3 4 1 2 3 4 1 2 3 4 1 2 3 4 1 2 3 4
> > > > > >

7. tap
count 1 2 3 4 1 2 3 4 1 2 3 4 1 2 3 4 1 2 3 4 1 2 3 4

8. tap
count 1 2 3 4 1 2 3 4 1 2 3 4 1 2 3 4 1 2 3 4 1 2 3 4

2 Rewrite the rhythms in **1** below the appropriate subdivision. Write the stems **down**.

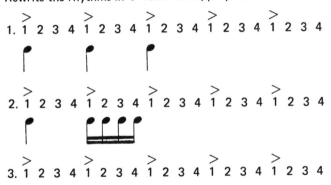

1. 1 2 3 4 1 2 3 4 1 2 3 4 1 2 3 4 1 2 3 4
   >   >   >   >   >

2. 1 2 3 4 1 2 3 4 1 2 3 4 1 2 3 4 1 2 3 4
   >   >   >   >   >

3. 1 2 3 4 1 2 3 4 1 2 3 4 1 2 3 4 1 2 3 4
   >   >   >   >   >

4. 1 2 3 4 1 2 3 4 1 2 3 4 1 2 3 4 1 2 3 4
   >   >   >   >   >

5. 1 2 3 4 1 2 3 4 1 2 3 4 1 2 3 4 1 2 3 4
   >   >   >   >   >

6. 1 2 3 4 1 2 3 4 1 2 3 4 1 2 3 4 1 2 3 4
   >   >   >   >   >

7. 1̲ 2 3 4 1̲ 2 3 4 1̲ 2 3 4 1̲ 2 3 4 1̲ 2 3 4

8. 1̲ 2 3 4 1̲ 2 3 4 1̲ 2 3 4 1̲ 2 3 4 1̲ 2 3 4

SUBDIVIDING INTO SIXTEENTHS, IN METER

When subdividing into sixteenths within a metered rhythm using the quarter note as the basic beat, the subdivision can be counted in this way: "one—ee—and—ee" (spoken slurred together with the accent on "one").

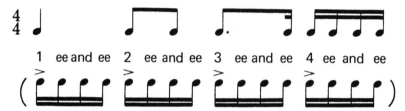

1   ee and ee   2   ee and ee   3   ee and ee   4   ee and ee

This method helps you keep track of the beat within the measure while still subdividing each beat into four parts.

3 Repeat **1**, using the "one—ee—and—ee" system.

4 Tap and count. The pulse equals the quarter note.

5. tap (right hand)

count 1 2 3 4 1 2 3 4 1 2 3 4 1 2 3 4 1 2 3 4

5 Tap with both hands:

1.
right hand

left hand

2.
right hand

left hand

3.
right hand

left hand

4.
right hand

left hand

5.
right hand

left hand

6.
right hand

left hand

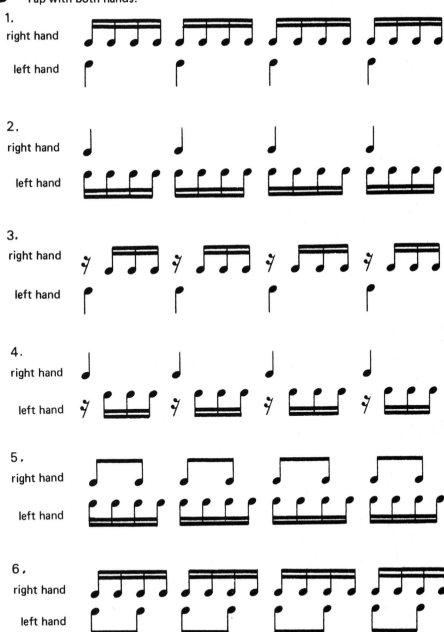

6 Tap and count:

1.

count 1 2 3 4 1 2 3 4 1 2 3 4 1 2 3 4 1 2 3 4
  >   >   >   >   >

2.

count 1 2 3 4 1 2 3 4 1 2 3 4 1 2 3 4 1 2 3 4
  >   >   >   >   >

3.

count 1 2 3 4 1 2 3 4 1 2 3 4 1 2 3 4 1 2 3 4
  >   >   >   >   >

4.

count 1 2 3 4 1 2 3 4 1 2 3 4 1 2 3 4 1 2 3 4 1 2 3 4
  >   >   >   >   >   >

7 Listen to *Rhythms 24–29.* Repeat, tapping the left-hand part only to get a sense of each rhythm. Repeat, tapping the right-hand part only. You may wish to work up to tapping both parts simultaneously. On the recording, the rhythms are grouped *24–26* (S 2, B 3) and *27–29* (S 2, B 4).

1. *Rhythm 24*

2. *Rhythm 25*

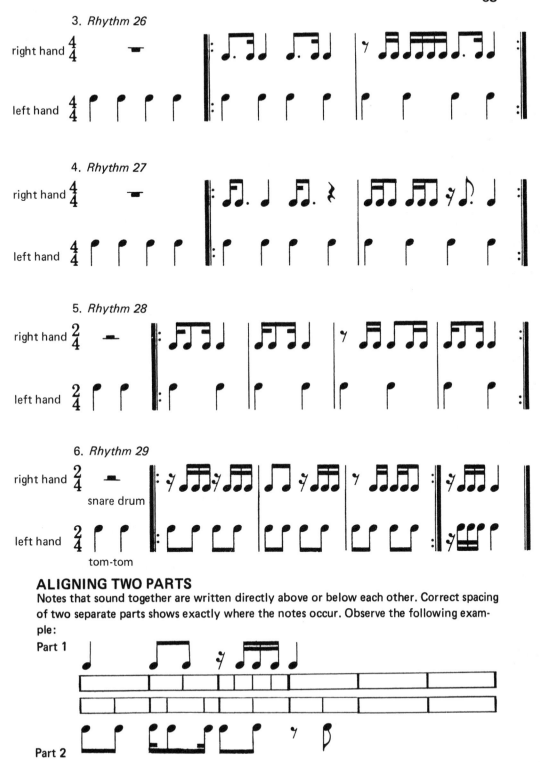

ALIGNING TWO PARTS

Notes that sound together are written directly above or below each other. Correct spacing of two separate parts shows exactly where the notes occur. Observe the following example:

Correctly aligned:

Part 1

Part 2

8 Put each rhythm on the rhythm spacer. Then copy the two parts again, using the rhythm spacer as a guide for aligning them correctly, as in the example above.

1.

Part 1    Part 2

Part 1

Part 2

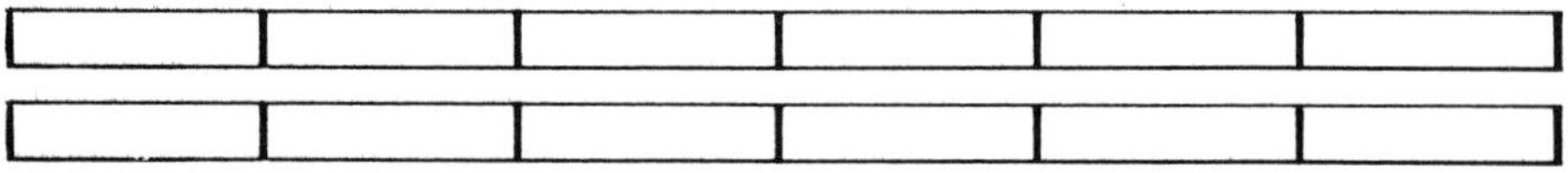

Part 1

Part 2

2.

Part 1    Part 2

Part 1

Part 2

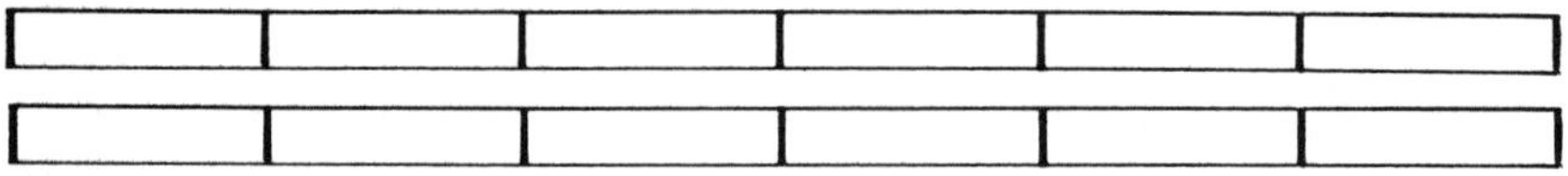

Part 1

Part 2

9 Play these exercises:

10 Play the following pieces from the *Scorebook*:

Alouette (SB 17)

Barbrie Allen (SB 9)

TERMS, SYMBOLS, AND CONCEPTS

subdivision into sixteenths

aligning rhythms

CHAPTER 9

COMPOUND METER

The meters we have studied so far have all utilized a basic pulse whose usual subdivision is two; such a meter is called a *simple meter.* However, there are meters whose basic pulse regularly subdivides into three parts; such a meter is called *compound meter.*

Simple meters

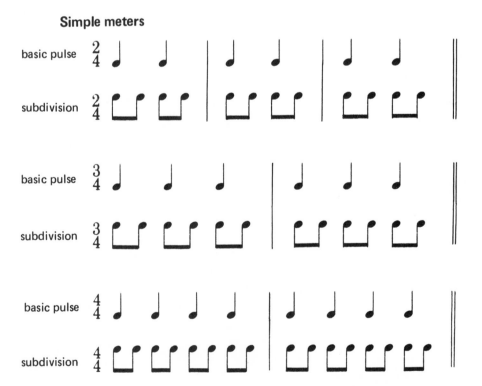

Compound meters

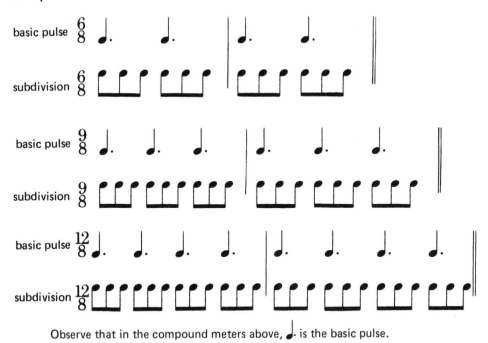

Observe that in the compound meters above, 𝅘𝅥𝅭. is the basic pulse.

1   Tap and count these rhythms:

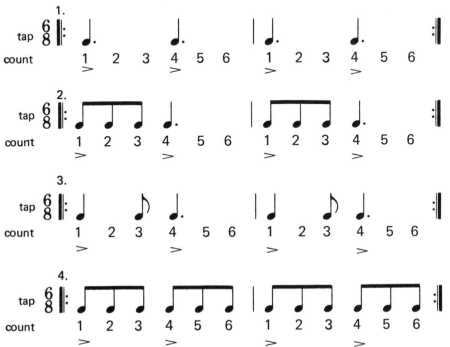

58

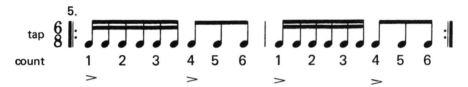

2 Tap and count these rhythms. First tap the left hand. Add the counting. Finally, add the right hand.

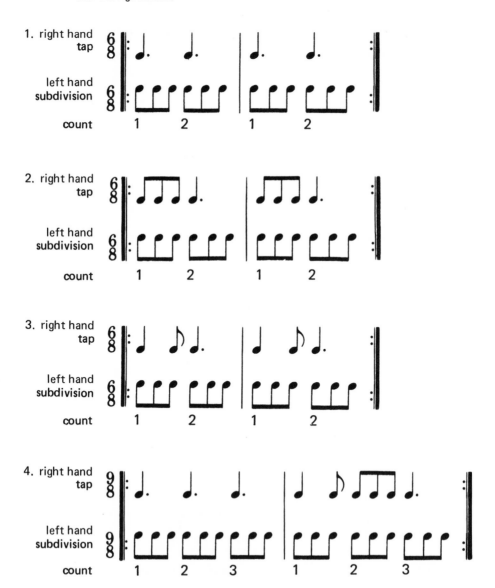

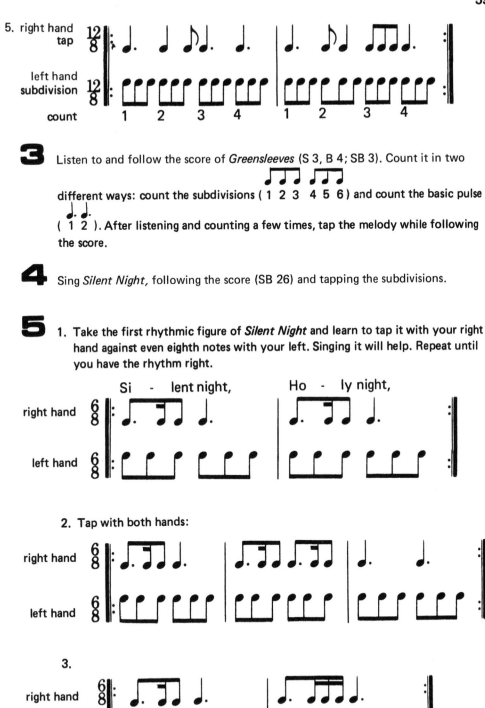

5. right hand tap

left hand subdivision

count

1 2 3 4 1 2 3 4

3 Listen to and follow the score of *Greensleeves* (S 3, B 4; SB 3). Count it in two

different ways: count the subdivisions (1 2 3 4 5 6) and count the basic pulse

(1 2). After listening and counting a few times, tap the melody while following the score.

4 Sing *Silent Night,* following the score (SB 26) and tapping the subdivisions.

5 1. Take the first rhythmic figure of *Silent Night* and learn to tap it with your right hand against even eighth notes with your left. Singing it will help. Repeat until you have the rhythm right.

Si - lent night,   Ho - ly night,

right hand

left hand

2. Tap with both hands:

right hand

left hand

3.

right hand

left hand

60

Listen to *Rhythms 30–32.* After you are familiar with the rhythmic structure, tap out the parts separately, then together. Repeat, counting the meter.

1. *Rhythm 30* (S 3, B 1)

2. *Rhythm 31* (S 3, B 1)

3. *Rhythm 32* (S 3, B 1)

ANOTHER WAY OF COUNTING

If you want to count aloud in compound meter and indicate both the basic pulse and the subdivision, it can be done in this way:

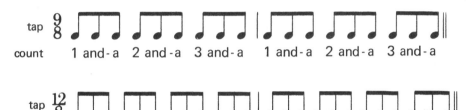

7 Play these exercises:

1.

2.

3.

8 Play these pieces in the *Scorebook*:

Drink to Me Only with Thine Eyes (SB 7)

Believe Me, If All Those Endearing Young Charms (SB 10)

TERMS. SYMBOLS, AND CONCEPTS

simple meter   counting in compound meter

compound meter

CHAPTER 10

TRIPLETS

Any note can be divided into three equal parts. Such a division is called a triplet. In this chapter, we will only consider the triplet division of the quarter note, which is notated

1 Tap *Rhythm 33* (S 3, B 2) with the recording.

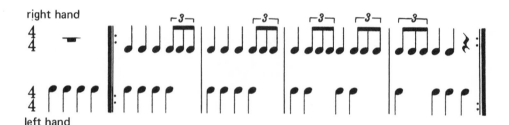

Observe how triplets are aligned on the rhythm spacer:

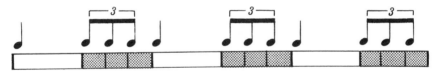

Compare the triplet with eighths:

Notice that only the use of a bracket and the number 3 (⌐—*3*—⌐) distinguishes eighth notes from triplets.

2 Align each pair of rhythms on the rhythm spacer, as indicated:

1. (a)

   (b)

2. (a)

   (b)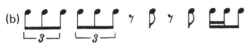

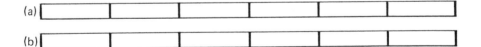

64

3. (a)

(b)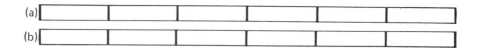

(a)

(b)

4. (a)

(b)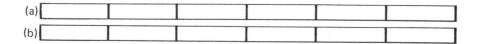

(a)

(b)

3 Tap both parts of *Rhythm 34* (S 3, B 2). Feel the difference between eighth notes and triplets.

right hand

left hand

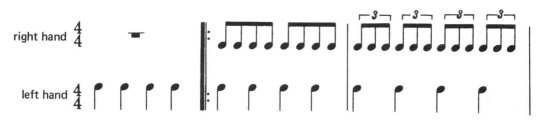

COUNTING TRIPLETS BY SUBDIVISION

The quarter note was subdivided into **two** equal parts by counting "1 and 2 and." The quarter note can be subdivided into **three** equal parts by counting "1 and—a 2 and—a 3 and—a 4 and—a."

4 Tap and count the top part of *Rhythm 34.*

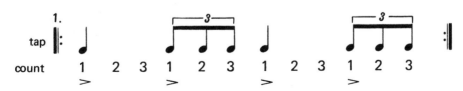

THE TRIPLET REST

When a rest occurs in the triplet subdivision, it is written like the eighth rest, but included within the triplet bracket.

5 Tap and count:

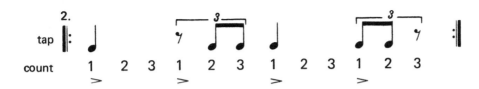

6   Tap the top part of *Rhythm 35* with the recording.

Rhythm 35 (S 3, B 2)

7   Tap the top part of the *Minuet* by Mozart (SB 40).

8   Play these exercises:

TERMS, SYMBOLS, AND CONCEPTS

┌─ *3* ─┐

triplet rest

CHAPTER 11

DIFFERENT VALUES OF THE BASIC PULSE

In the rhythms we have studied so far, the basic pulse has been represented by ♩ or ♩. Other rhythmic values can be used as the basic pulse, depending on the tempo, the historical period in which a piece was composed, or the whim of the composer. Observe these examples:

C AND ¢

C the symbol for common time, represents $\frac{4}{4}$.

¢ (*alla breve* sign) indicates a halving of the time values, thus changing **C** ($\frac{4}{4}$) to **¢** ($\frac{2}{2}$).

(basic pulse: ♩)   (basic pulse: ♩)

Changing the ratio of note values can go either way, as illustrated by this example:

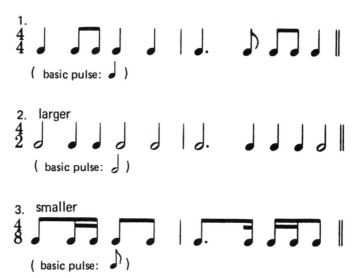

1.

(basic pulse: ♩)

2. larger

(basic pulse: ♩)

3. smaller

(basic pulse: ♪)

All three rhythms sound exactly alike, if the **tempo** (rate of speed) of the basic pulse is the same. Notice that example 2 is created by doubling the original quarter-note pulse, while example 3 is created by dividing the original quarter-note pulse in half.

1   Tap out *Rhythm 17* (S 2, B 1) with the recording, first in its original form, then in the two other versions.

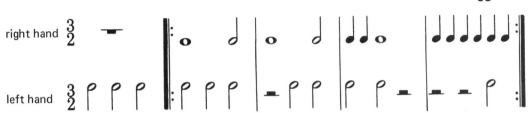

2 Write the following rhythm two other ways, as in the example above. Tap it three times.

3 Tap *Rhythm 33* (S 3, B 2) with the recording, according to these three versions.

TRIPLETS WITH DIFFERENT NOTE VALUES

Notice that triplets can be written with any note value, not just the quarter note. Dotted notes (for example ♪. ♩. 𝅗𝅥.) can be divided into three without the triplet sign. For example:

Notes that are not dotted can be divided into two parts without special notation, but require a triplet indication to be divided into three parts. Compare the following:

4 Tap out the rhythm of *Greensleeves* (S 3, B 4) with the recording. Follow the original version (1) for the first verse. Follow the alternative notation (2) for the second verse.

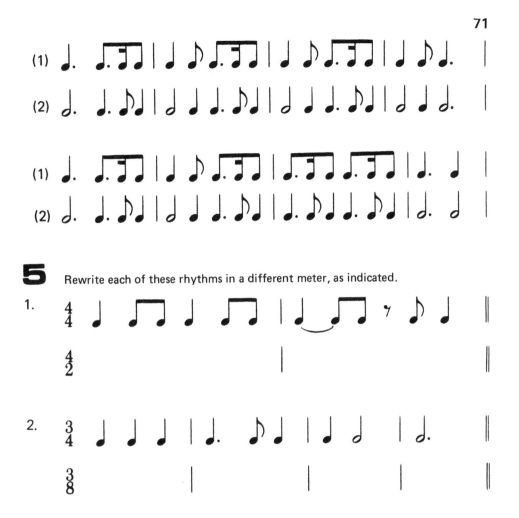

5 Rewrite each of these rhythms in a different meter, as indicated.

TERMS, SYMBOLS, AND CONCEPTS

using different note values for the basic pulse

𝄴 and 𝄵

doubling the value of the basic pulse

dividing the value of the basic pulse

triplets with different note values

CHAPTER 12

In the following examples, you may wish to speak the rhythms. These exercises are somewhat tricky and speaking them will be helpful. First learn the rhythms.

1   Speak *Rhythms 36–39* with the recordings.

Rhythm 36 (S 3, B 3)

Rhythm 37 (S 3, B 3)

Rhythm 38 (S 3, B 3)

Rhythm 39 (S 3, B 3)

SYNCOPATED AND NONSYNCOPATED RHYTHMS

Notes can occur **on** the beat or **off** the beat.

On the beat

Off the beat

Rhythms that have accented notes off the beat are said to be *syncopated.*
Rhythms 36-39 (page 72) are all syncopated.

Syncopated rhythm

Nonsyncopated

2 Line up these rhythms on the rhythm spacer:

1.

2.

3.

VISUALIZING WHERE THE BEAT FALLS

To understand a complex rhythm, you must be able to visualize where the beat occurs.

rhythm

imaginary beat

An easy way to indicate the beat is to draw a line where the basic beat occurs.

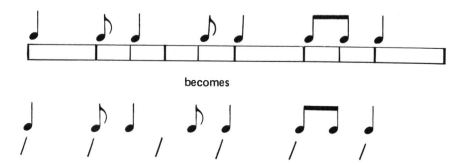

rhythm

imaginary beat

These marks locate the beat in the same way that the rhythm spacer does.

becomes

3 Mark where the quarter-note beat falls.
Example

1.

2.

3.

4.

5.

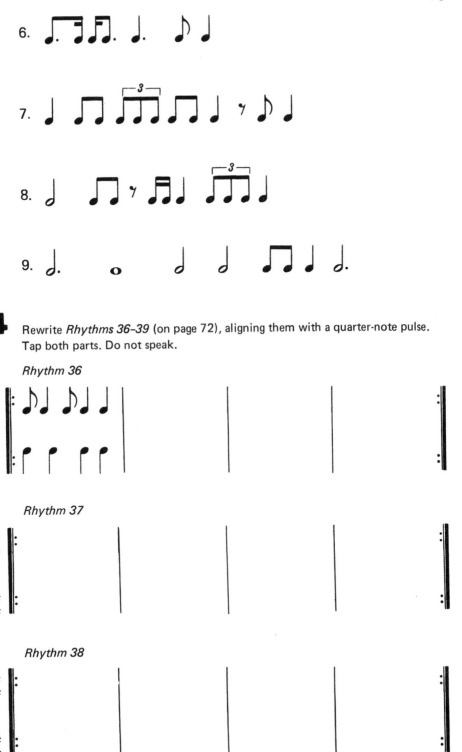

4 Rewrite *Rhythms 36–39* (on page 72), aligning them with a quarter-note pulse. Tap both parts. Do not speak.

Rhythm 39

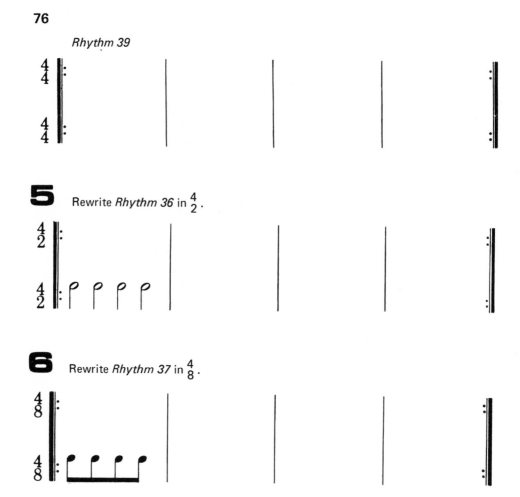

5 Rewrite *Rhythm 36* in $\frac{4}{2}$.

6 Rewrite *Rhythm 37* in $\frac{4}{8}$.

TERMS, SYMBOLS, AND CONCEPTS

syncopation

visualizing where the beat occurs

SCOREBOOK

THE TREES THEY DO GROW HIGH

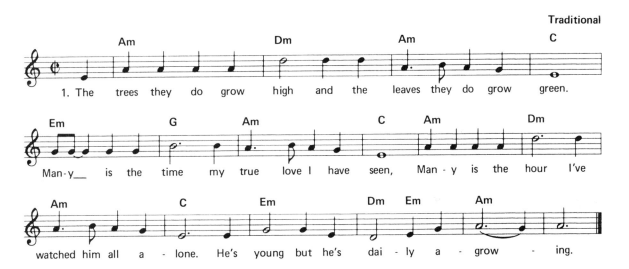

Traditional

1. The trees they do grow high and the leaves they do grow green. Man-y__ is the time my true love I have seen, Man - y is the hour I've watched him all a - lone. He's young but he's dai - ly a - grow - ing.

2. Father, dear Father, you've done me great wrong,
   You've married me to a boy who is too young.
   I am twice twelve and he is but fourteen,
   He's young, but he's daily a-growing.

3. Daughter, dear daughter, I've done you no wrong,
   I've married you to a great lord's son.
   He will make a lord for you to wait upon,
   He's young, but he's daily a-growing.

4. At the age of fourteen, he was a married man,
   At the age of fifteen, the father of a son,
   At the age of sixteen, his grave it did grow green,
   And death put an end to his growing.

2 I KNOW WHERE I'M GOING

Traditional

1. I know where I'm go - ing, and I know who's go - ing with me; I know who I love, but the dear knows who I'll mar - ry. 2. Feath - er beds are soft, and paint - ed rooms are bon - nie; But I would trade them all for my hand - some, win - some John - nie.

3. I have stockings of silk, and shoes of bright green leather;
   Combs to buckle my hair, and a ring for every finger.

4. Some say he's bad, but I say he's bonnie;
   Fairest of them all is my handsome, winsome Johnnie.

③ GREENSLEEVES

Traditional

A - las, my love,___ you do me wrong___ To cast me off___ dis -
cour - teous - ly, And I have lov - ed you so long,___ De - light - ing in___ your
com - pa - ny. Green - sleeves___ was all my joy,____ Green - sleeves___ was my de - light,
Green - sleeves was my heart of gold___ And who but my la - dy Green - sleeves.

4 ONE GRAIN OF SAND

Appalachian Lullaby

Rhythm freely improvised

1. One grain of sand,_____ one grain of sand_____ in all the world;
One grain of sand,_____ one lit-tle boy, one lit-tle girl.

2. One drop of rain, one drop of rain on all the land;
   One drop of rain, one little hand in all my hand.

3. One little star, one little star up in the blue;
   One little star, one little me, one little you.

4. One grain of sand, one grain of sand in all the world;
   One grain of sand, one little boy, one little girl.

5 THE WATER IS WIDE

Traditional

The wa-ter is wide,_____ I can-not get o'er,_____ and nei-ther

have_____ I_____ wings to fly._____ Give me a boat_____

_ that can car - ry two,_____ and both shall row,_____ my love and I._____

2. I leaned my back against an oak,
   Thinking it was a trusty tree;
   But first it bended and then it broke,
   As thus did my true love to me.

6 THE RIDDLE SONG

Traditional

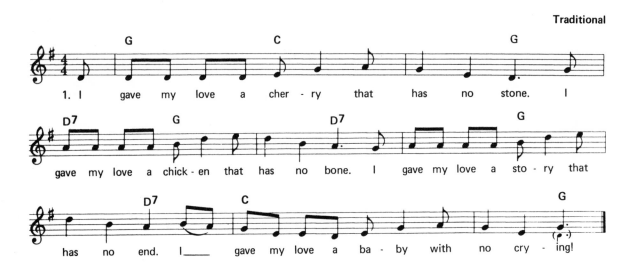

1. I gave my love a cher - ry that has no stone. I gave my love a chick - en that has no bone. I gave my love a sto - ry that has no end. I___ gave my love a ba - by with no cry - ing!

2. How can there be a cherry that has no stone?
   How can there be a chicken that has no bone?
   How can there be a story that has no end?
   How can there be a baby with no crying?

3. A cherry when its blooming, it has no stone.
   A chicken when its pipping, it has no bone.
   The story of "I love you," it has no end.
   A baby when its sleeping, there's no crying.

7 DRINK TO ME ONLY WITH THINE EYES

Words by Ben Jonson (1616)

Traditional English

Drink to me on - ly with_ thine eyes,_ And I___ will pledge with mine;___

Or leave a kiss but in__ the cup,_ And I'll__ not ask for wine.___ The

thirst_ that from the soul__ doth rise, Doth ask a drink_ di - vine:____

But might I of Jove's nec - tar sup,__ I would_ not change for thine.___

2. I sent thee late a rosy wreath,
   Not so much honoring thee,
   As giving it a hope, that there
   It could not withered be.
   But thou thereon did'st only breathe,
   And sent'st it back to me;
   Since when it grows and smells, I swear,
   Not of itself, but thee.

⑧ LULLABY

Johannes Brahms
1833–1897

⑨ BARBRIE ALLEN

Traditional English

1. In Scar-let-town where I was born, There was a fair maid dwell-ing, Made
ev-'ry youth cry__ "Well a - day," Her name was Bar - brie Al - len.

2. All in the merry month of May,
   When green buds they were swelling,
   Young Jonny Grove on his deathbed lay,
   For love of Barbrie Allen.

3. He sent his man unto her then
   To the town where she was dwelling:
   "You must come to my master, dear,
   If your name be Barbrie Allen."

4. So slowly, slowly she came up,
   And slowly she came nigh him,
   And all she said when there she came:
   "Young man, I think you're dying!"

5. He turned his face unto the wall,
   And death was drawing nigh him:
   "Adieu, adieu, my dear friends all,
   Be kind to Barbrie Allen."

10 BELIEVE ME, IF ALL THOSE ENDEARING YOUNG CHARMS

Words by Thomas Moore (1808)   Traditional

Be - lieve me, if all those en - dear-ing young charms, Which I gaze on so fond - ly to -

day,____ Were to change by to - mor - row, and fleet in my arms, Like__

fair - y gifts fad - ing a - way,____ Thou wouldst still be a - dored, as this

mo - ment thou art, Let thy love - li - ness fade as it will,____ And a -

round the dear ru - in, each wish of my heart, Would en - twine it - self ver - dant-ly still.____

11 DOWN IN THE VALLEY

Traditional American

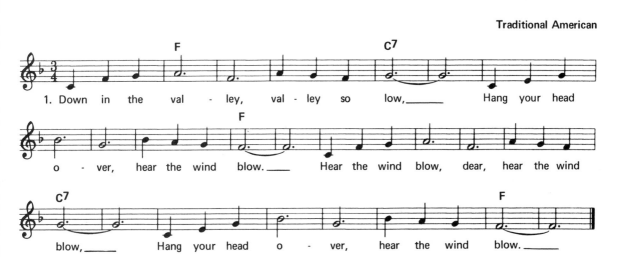

1. Down in the val - ley, val - ley so low,_____ Hang your head o - ver, hear the wind blow._____ Hear the wind blow, dear, hear the wind blow,_____ Hang your head o - ver, hear the wind blow._____

2. Writing this letter, containing three lines,
   Answer my question, will you be mine?
   Will you be mine, dear, will you be mine?
   Answer my question, will you be mine?

3. Roses love sunshine, violets love dew,
   Angels in heaven know I love you.
   Know I love you, dear, know I love you,
   Angels in heaven know I love you.

12 DONA, DONA

Traditional Hebrew

13 BLACK, BLACK, BLACK

Traditional American

1. Black, black, black is the col - or of my true love's hair; Her
lips___ are some-thing won - drous fair; The___ cool - est___ brow and the
dain - ti - est hands; I love_____ the grass where - on she stands.

2. I love my love and well she knows,
   I love the ground whereon she goes.
   If she no more on earth I'd see,
   My life would quickly leave me.

14 WAYFARING STRANGER

Traditional American

I'm just a poor__ way-far-ing stran-ger,__ A-trav-'ling through__ this world of woe,__ And there's no sick - ness,toil, or dan-ger__ In that bright land__ to which I go.__ I'm go-ing there__ to meet my moth-er,__ I'm go-ing there__ no more to roam.__ I'm just a-go - ing o-ver Jor-dan,__ I'm just a-go - ing o-ver home.__

15 THE WRAGGLE-TAGGLE GYPSIES, O!

Traditional English

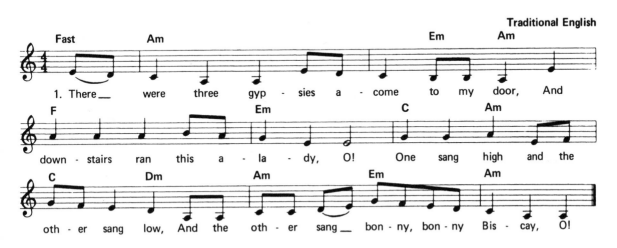

1. There __ were three gyp - sies a - come to my door, And down - stairs ran this a - la - dy, O! One sang high and the oth - er sang low, And the oth - er sang __ bon - ny, bon - ny Bis - cay, O!

2. Then she pulled off her silk-finished gown,
   And put on hose of leather, O!
   The ragged, ragged rags about our door,
   And she's gone with the wraggle-taggle Gypsies, O!

3. It was late last night when my lord came home,
   Inquiring for his lady, O!
   The servants cried on every hand,
   She's gone with the wraggle-taggle Gypsies, O!

4. O, saddle to me my milk-white steed,
   And go and fetch me my pony, O!
   That I may ride to seek my bride,
   Who is gone with the wraggle-taggle Gypsies, O!

5. O, he rode high, and he rode low,
   He rode through wood and copses, too,
   Until he came to a wide open field,
   And there he espied his a-lady, O!

6. "What makes you leave your house and land?
   What makes you leave your money, O!
   What makes you leave your new-wedded lord,
   To follow the wraggle-taggle Gypsies, O!"

7. "What care I for my house and my land?
   What care I for my money, O?
   What care I for my new-wedded lord?
   I'm off with the wraggle-taggle Gypsies, O!"

16 JOHNNY HAS GONE FOR A SOLDIER

Traditional American

1. There I sat on But-ter-milk Hill, Who could blame me weep my fill, And
eve-ry tear would turn a mill: John-ny has gone for a sol-dier.

2. Me, oh my, I loved him so,
Broke my heart to see him go,
And only time will heal my woe:
Johnny has gone for a soldier.

17 ALOUETTE

Refrain

French-Canadian Game Song

A - lou - et - te, gen - tille A - lou - et - te, A - lou - et - te, je te plu - me-rai. 1. Je te plu - me - rai la tête, je te plu - me - rai la tête.

Et la tête, et la tête, A - lou - ette, Oh

2. Je te plumerai le cou, *etc.*

3. Je te plumerai les ailes, *etc.*

4. Je te plumerai les pattes, *etc.*

5. Je te plumerai le dos, *etc.*

6. Je te plumerai la queue, *etc.*

*Repeat all previous verses in reverse order. The last verse will end, "Et la queue, et le dos, et les pattes, et les ailes, et le cou, et la tête."

18 GO DOWN, MOSES

Spiritual

Verse

1. When Is - rael was in E - gypt's land, Let my peo - ple
go. Op - pressed so hard they could not stand, Let my peo - ple go.

Refrain

Go down, Mo - ses, way down in E - gypt's land,_____
Tell___ old Pha - raoh to let my peo - ple go.

2. Thus spake the Lord, bold Moses said,
   Let my people go.
   If not, I'll smite your first-born dead,
   Let my people go.
   Go down, Moses, way down in Egypt's land,
   Tell old Pharaoh to let my people go.

19 CHERRY BLOOMS

Traditional Japanese

20 ALL THE BEAUTY WITHIN YOU

Traditional Italian

1. All beau - ty with - in you, all gra - ces a - round you, So

late I have found you, so soon we must part! Ah, no, no, no, weep not, take

cour - age, my beau - ty, To go__ is__ my__ du - ty, I leave you my heart.

2. I swear to return you the life you have lent me,
No force shall prevent me, not Death with his dart.
Ah no, no, no, weep not, take courage, my beauty,
To go is my duty, I leave you my heart.

21 JEUNE FILLETTE

Traditional French

22 PHILIS, PLUS AVARE QUE TENDRE

Traditional French

23 QUE NE SUIS-JE LA FOUGÈRE

Traditional French

24 MELODY

Traditional Finnish

25 HO THERE, BROTHER

Traditional Yugoslavian

26 SILENT NIGHT

Words by Joseph Mohn

Franz Gruber

Si - lent night, ho - ly night, All is calm, all is bright.

Round yon Vir - gin Moth - er and Child, Ho - ly In - fant so ten - der and mild,

Sleep in heav - en - ly peace,___ sleep___ in heav - en - ly peace.

27 THE FIRST NOEL

Traditional Carol

The __ first __ No - el, the __ an - gels did say, Was to cer - tain poor

shep - herds in fields as they lay; In __ fields __ where __ they lay __ keep - ing their

sheep, On a cold win - ter's night __ that was __ so deep. No - el, __ No -

el, No - el, No - el, Born is the King __ of Is - ra - el.

28 OH, HOW LOVELY IS THE EVENING

German Round

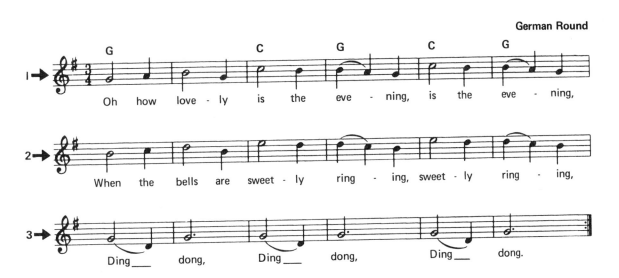

29 HEY, HO, NOBODY AT HOME

English Round (1609)

Hey, Ho, no-bod-y at home,

Food nor drink nor mon-ey have we none,

Yet shall we be mer - ry. ___

30 DONA NOBIS PACEM

Traditional Round

31 SHALOM CHAVERIM

Israeli Round

Sha - lom cha - ve - rim, sha - lom cha - ve - rim, sha - lom, sha -

lom, Le hit - ra - ot, le hit - ra - ot, sha - lom, sha - lom.

32 THE WELCOME SONG

18th-Century American Canon

Wel - come, wel - come eve - ry guest, wel - come to our mu - sic fest.

Mu - sic is our on - ly___ cheer, fills both soul and___ ra - vished ear.

Sa - cred nine___teach us the mood, sweet - est notes to___ be ex - plored.

Gen - tly moves the trem - bling_ air to_ com - plete our_ con - cert fair.

33 VICTIMAE PASCHALI

Gregorian Chant

Wipo
(c. 1000–1050)

Vi - cti - mae pa - scha - li lau - des im - mo - lent Chri - sti - a - ni

A - gnus red - e - mit o - ves: Chri - stus in - no - cens Pa - tri

re - con - ci - li - a - vit pec - ca - to - res.

34 THE YOUNG CONVERT

19th-Century New England Hymn

35 WILLIE, TAKE YOUR LITTLE DRUM

Burgundian Carol
Arranged by L. Shelton

1. Willie, take your little drum, With your whistle Robin, come! When we hear the fife and drum, Turelurelu patapata pan, When we hear the fife and drum, Christmas should be frolicsome.

2. God and man are now become
More than one with fife and drum.
When you hear the fife and drum,
Turelurelu, patapatapan,
When you hear the fife and drum,
Dance, and make the village hum!

36 REMEMBER, O THOU MAN

A Christmas Carol

Thomas Ravenscroft
(c. 1590-1663)

2. Remember God's goodnesse,
   O thou man, O thou man
   Remember God's goodnesse
   And his promise made.
   Remember God's goodnesse,
   How he sent his son doubtlesse
   Our sinnes for to redresse, be not affraid.

3. The Angels all did sing,
   O thou man, O thou man,
   The Angels all did sing
   Upon Shepheards hill.
   The Angels all did sing
   Praises to our heavenly King,
   And peace to man living with a good will.

37 SARABANDA

Arcangelo Corelli
(1653–1713)

From Concerto Grosso, Opus 6, No. 11 (melody only)

38 MINUET FOR LUTE

Robert Visée
(c. 1650–c. 1725)

Melody only

39 MINUET

Henry Purcell
(c. 1659–1695)

Melody only

40 MINUET K.2

Wolfgang Amadeus Mozart
(1756–1791)

41 STUDY IN C

For Guitar (excerpt)

Fernando Sor
(1778–1839)

42 ODE TO JOY

From Symphony No. 9 in D Major (melody only)

Ludwig van Beethoven
(1770–1827)

43 DEMONSTRATION MELODY 1

a.

b.

c.

d.

44 DEMONSTRATION MELODY 2

a.

b.

c.

d.

* Try both ♮ and ♭ on 6th degree.